You're A Pal, Snoopy!

You're a Pal, Snoopy!

by Charles M. Schulz

Selected cartoons from
You Need Help, Charlie Brown, Volume 2

A FAWCETT CREST BOOK

Fawcett Publications, Inc., Greenwich, Conn.

YOU'RE A PAL, SNOOPY!

This book, prepared especially for Fawcett Publications, Inc., comprises the second half of YOU NEED HELP, CHARLIE BROWN, and is reprinted by arrangement with Holt, Rinehart & Winston, Inc.

Printed in the United States of America

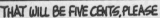

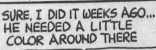

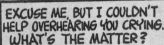

DEAR MOM AND DAD, THINGS ARE GOING BETTER HERE AT CAMP.

Yesterday I met this kid named Charlie Brown.

HE WAS VERY LONESOME, BUT I THINK I HAVE HELPED HIM.

He's the kind who makes a good temporary friend.

SCHULZ

WELL, SO LONG, CHARLIE BROWN... IT'S BEEN NICE KNOWING YOU..

IT'S BEEN NICE KNOWING YOU, TOO, ROY....HAVE A GOOD TRIP HOME..

FOR THE FIRST TIME IN MY LIFE I FEEL I REALLY HELPED SOMEONE...HE WAS LONESOME, AND I BECAME HIS FRIEND...

WHAT AN ACCOMPLISHMENT!

SCHULZ

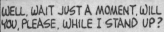

WHY DID YOU WRITE, "CHARLIE BROWN IS A BLOCKHEAD" ON THE SIDEWALK?

BECAUSE I SINCERELY BELIEVE YOU ARE A BLOCKHEAD! I HAVE TO WRITE WHAT I BELIEVE IS TRUE.. IT'S MY MORAL RESPONSIBILITY!

DEEP DOWN I ADMIRE HER INTEGRITY..

SCHULZ

IT'S A GOOD THUMB, BUT NOT A GREAT THUMB!

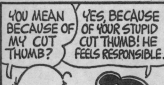

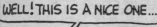

DEAR GREAT PUMPKIN, SOMETHING HAS OCCURRED TO ME.

YOU MUST GET DISCOURAGED BECAUSE MORE PEOPLE BELIEVE IN SANTA CLAUS THAN IN YOU.

WELL, LET'S FACE IT... SANTA CLAUS HAS HAD MORE PUBLICITY.

BUT BEING NUMBER TWO, PERHAPS YOU TRY HARDER.

SCHULZ.

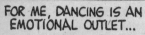

ONLY 6
DAYS
UNTIL...
BEETHOVEN'S
BIRTHDAY

ELEVEN
DAYS TO
THE FIRST
DAY OF
WINTER

ONLY 12
SHOPPING
DAYS UNTIL
CHRISTMAS

IT'S UNUSUAL FOR ONE AGENCY
TO HAVE ALL THREE ACCOUNTS!